LEGO STAR WARS

DEFENDERS
—OF THE—
REPUBLIC

INTRODUCTION

The democratic Republic peacefully governs the LEGO® *Star Wars* galaxy. Discover all about this amazing group— from the beautiful Padmé Naberrie to the courageous Captain Rex.

HOW TO USE THIS BOOK

These amazing minifigures are ordered according to the *Star Wars*® property in which they first appeared or mostly featured. Tabs at the top of each page indicate which properties this minifgure appears in. As most Star Wars characters appear in the Expanded Universe, that tab is highlighted only if a minifigure appears in an EU set. The Clone Wars tab has not been highlighted if the character has a separate Clone Wars minifigure.

This book also includes variants of featured minifigures, which are the same character, but have some modifications that make them different in some way.

Contents

Bumbling Gungan Jar Jar Binks broke the LEGO mold as the first minifigure ever to have a unique head sculpt. He found his way into five Episode I sets in 1999–2000, and then made a comeback in the 2011 set The Battle of Naboo (7929). In 2011, Jar Jar's head-mold had printing added to it to give him a new look.

Flat eyes, painted yellow with black pupils

STAR VARIANT

Early Jar Jar
The first LEGO Jar Jar Binks has a very similar head-mold to the 2011 design except for one thing: his eye stalks are split to depict his eyes. On the 2011 design, Jar Jar's eye stalks are flat and he has painted eyes.

Mottled skin is good for camouflage

Amphibious ears
Jar Jar's distinct floppy ears are integrated into his head-mold and are printed with a mottled-skin pattern.

Jar Jar Binks
GOOFY GUNGAN

Jar Jar is an outcast from his people and lives alone in the swamps, so his clothing is dirty and ragged

Torso design is first seen on the 2011 design. The pattern continues on the back

This Jar Jar has flesh-colored arms and hands, while the original has lighter tan arms and hands

DATA FILE
SET: 7929 The Battle of Naboo
YEAR: 2011
PIECES: 3
EQUIPMENT: Energy balls
VARIANTS: 2

STAR VARIANT

First Queen
The original Padmé Naberrie minifigure has yellow flesh, a unique wide-smiled head, and slightly different printing on her torso. She comes in two sets: Anakin's Podracer (set 7131) and Mos Espa Podrace (set 7171).

Two faces
One side of Padmé's face is smiling, but turn it around and the other side has a look of concern.

Padmé's long hair is braided at the top and flows down her back

Don't tell anyone but Padmé Naberrie is actually Queen Amidala of Naboo in disguise! She is dressed as one of her handmaidens to avoid detection on the planet Tatooine. Padmé appears in this disguise in three LEGO *Star Wars* sets, in two variations, but she remains an enigma in the LEGO world—she has never been seen in her royal robes as Queen of Naboo.

Padmé is simply dressed in a gray vest and blue undershirt. This unique torso pattern continues on the back

Red-jeweled belt

Padmé carries a short blaster pistol to protect herself

Padmé Naberrie
DISGUISED QUEEN OF NABOO

DATA FILE
SET: 7961 Darth Maul's Sith Infiltrator
YEAR: 2011
PIECES: 4
EQUIPMENT: Blaster
VARIANTS: 2

7

Anakin Skywalker
PODRACING SLAVE BOY

Young slave Anakin Skywalker may be just a boy, but he can handle a Podracer like no one else! This minifigure made his Podracing debut in 1999 and has since sped into seven sets. The 2011 variant can change from ordinary slave boy to Podracing supremo, ready to ride in his redesigned Podracer.

Anakin's Podracer (set 7131)

Look out for Anakin's Podracer swooshing through the skies! Seated in the control pod of this 1999 set is the original Anakin, with regular (not short) legs and a gray helmet. Anakin's Podracer was updated in 2011.

The variant in the Naboo Starfighter (set 7877) has a brown helmet and hair

STAR VARIANT

Short stuff
The young Anakin minifigure was one of the first to try out shorter legs. The first variant seen with them is in the 2007 set Naboo N-1 Starfighter and Vulture Droid (7660).

Rare racer
This early variant is exclusive to the 1999 set Naboo Starfighter (7141). A similar variant with a gray helmet appears in three 1999–2000 sets.

DATA FILE
SET: 7962 Anakin's and Sebulba's Podracers
YEAR: 2011
PIECES: 4
EQUIPMENT: None
VARIANTS: 4

Necklace given to Anakin by his mother

Anakin wears a simple slave tunic with a brown belt on Tatooine. His clothing can be seen on the back of his torso, too

The shorter LEGO legs do not have a moveable hip joint like regular legs

Podrace face
This side of Anakin's face has goggles and a determined look. He is ready to Podrace!

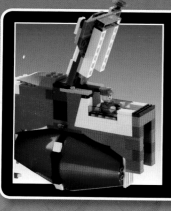

Republic Cruiser (set 7665)
The Republic captain is in command of the Republic Cruiser *Radiant VII*. He runs the starship from a control panel inside its middle section and leaves the job of flying it to the Republic pilot (pictured). The Republic pilot sits in the cockpit, which has room for just one minifigure.

The smartly dressed Republic captain minifigure appears in only one LEGO set, flying alongside the almost identical Republic pilot. As captain of the imposing Republic Cruiser (set 7665), the minifigure is charged with the mission of safely shuttling Jedi Obi-Wan Kenobi and Qui-Gon Jinn across the galaxy to Naboo.

Light flesh head with standard grin pattern

This blue crew uniform is unique to the Republic captain and pilot of the Republic Cruiser

Republic Pilot
The Republic pilot is exactly the same minifigure as the Republic captain but he has a blue hat instead of hair.

Silver belt buckle

Dark-blue hips and legs

DATA FILE
SET: 7665 Republic Cruiser
YEAR: 2007
PIECES: 4
EQUIPMENT: None
VARIANTS: 1

Maoi Madakor?
The Republic captain minifigure may be the female captain of *Radiant VII* Maoi Madakor, as seen in Episode I —although it is not named as her by the LEGO Group. The Republic pilot may be her co-pilot Antidar Williams.

Republic Captain
CRUISER COMMANDER

Working away behind the scenes on the Republic Cruiser (set 7665) is R2-R7. If you blink you might miss him, as this green astromech droid has only ever been seen in one LEGO set. He has a docking station aboard the starship from which he provides indispensible in-flight backup for the Republic captain and pilot minifigures.

Republic Cruiser (set 7665)

The dependable R2-R7 is exclusive to this one 2007 set. The astromech droid has a docking station in the command center within the middle interior of the ship. He sits alongside the Republic captain, providing in-flight support.

R2-R7
GREEN ASTROMECH DROID

DATA FILE
SET: 7665 Republic Cruiser
YEAR: 2007
PIECES: 4
EQUIPMENT: None
VARIANTS: 1

Radar eye tracks flight paths and scans for malfunctions

Silver and green printed head. The only other green astromech droid is R4-P44 (p.25)

Ghost droid
R2-R7 was obviously very hard at work aboard the Republic Cruiser in Episode I because he was never actually seen in the movie! His role is to monitor flight performance and carry out repairs.

R2-R7's legs are moveable because they are attached to his body piece with LEGO Technic pins

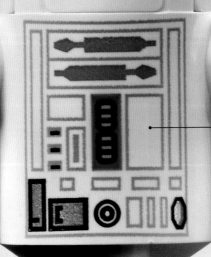

These compartments house tools and connectors that mean R2-R7 can fix just about anything

Protruding lower body stores a third leg for extra maneuverability

STAR VARIANT

Green Gungan

This was the first variant into battle in LEGO *Star Wars*. He is exclusive to the 2000 set Gungan Patrol (set 7115). His plain head is the same as that seen on the first Jar Jar Binks (p.6), and his uniform is green instead of brown.

This head-mold is the same as that on the Jar Jar Binks minifigure (p.6), with different printing

Combat eye mask

The Gungans are a peaceful people, but when Naboo is deluged by the Trade Federation's droid army, they are forced to wage war to protect it. The Gungan soldier has battled in two LEGO *Star Wars* sets, and due to a 2011 redesign, the minifigures in each set are different.

DATA FILE

SET: 7929 Battle of Naboo
YEAR: 2011
PIECES: 3
EQUIPMENT: Cesta and energy ball, energy shield
VARIANTS: 2

This cesta has an energy ball mounted on it, ready to be hurled at a battle droid

Brown uniform is first seen on the 2011 design. Many Gungan soldiers are part-time and provide their own uniforms—which might explain the difference in uniform on both variants

Unique energy shield protects the Gungan soldier from blaster fire

Gungan garb

The Gungan soldier's primitive Grand Army uniform and gold belt can be seen on the back of his torso as well as the front.

Gungan Soldier
AMPHIBIOUS FIGHTER

This pilot of peaceful Naboo is not used to conflict, but when the Trade Federation invades his planet, he must take action to defend it in his N-1 starfighter! The pacifist pilot minifigure never carries a weapon, but his 2011 redesign finds himself bound with handcuffs when he is captured by security battle droid minifigures.

Naboo Starfighter (set 7877)

The latest variant of the Naboo fighter pilot appears in this 2011 set. The minifigure can pilot a fast and agile N-1 starfighter—if young Anakin Skywalker's minifigure hasn't already taken off in it!

Naboo Fighter Pilot
INFREQUENT FLIER

Reddish-brown flying helmet with removeable goggles

Unique torso features a safety harness, flying jacket and undershirt, and a red overcoat

DATA FILE

SET: 7877 Naboo Starfighter
YEAR: 2011
PIECES: 5
EQUIPMENT: ~~Handcuffs~~
VARIANTS: 2

Reddish-brown flying gloves

STAR VARIANT

First look
The Naboo pilot in the Naboo N-1 Starfighter and Vulture Droid (set 7660) looks different to his 2011 counterpart. He wears a brown cap, tan flying jacket, and reddish-brown pants.

Full-length Space Fighter Corps overcoat

12

Sith Infiltrator (set 7961)

Captain Panaka's minifigure is exclusive to this 2011 set. Deadly Sith apprentice Darth Maul is in pursuit of Captain Panaka and his charge, Queen Padmé Amidala, in his Sith Infiltrator. Can the minifigures escape Maul?

A great deal of responsibility rests on this minifigure's shoulders. Captain Panaka is Head of the Royal Naboo Security Forces. He is also solely responsible for the Queen's safety. Dressed in a distinctive Naboo High Officer uniform, the minifigure makes his first and only appearance in the Sith Infiltrator (set 7961).

Unique gold and red LEGO helmet bears the Naboo Security crest

Captain Panaka has a unique LEGO head. His stern expression shows how seriously he takes his responsibilities as Head of Security

As a Naboo High Officer, Panaka wears a protective jerkin with inbuilt anti-blast armor plates

Protective reddish-brown gloves

Captain Panaka
NABOO HEAD OF SECURITY

DATA FILE

SET: 7961 Darth Maul's Sith Infiltrator
YEAR: 2011
PIECES: 4
EQUIPMENT: Blaster
VARIANTS: 1

13

This smiling security guard patrols the peaceful planet of Naboo. The minifigure is rarely called into combat, so he carries no weapons. When Naboo is invaded by the Trade Federation, he is forced to use his Flash Speeder (set 7124) in battle—but he might need to arm himself with more than his binoculars!

Flash Speeder (set 7124)

The Naboo security officer is exclusive to this 2000 set. He pilots the repulsorlift craft with a joystick and control panel. He places his electrobinoculars in a storage compartment during flight.

Naboo Security Officer
INVADED INFANTRYMAN

Brown guard cap

DATA FILE

SET: 7124 Flash Speeder
YEAR: 2000
PIECES: 4
EQUIPMENT: Electro-binoculars
VARIANTS: 1

The Imperial officer, Dak Ralter, and the Imperial pilot also have this yellow LEGO head

Naboo security guards wear distinctive brown and tan uniforms

Protective gloves

Headgear
The Naboo security officer's hat is a popular one among LEGO minifigures, but only he wears it in brown. In LEGO *Star Wars*, the Imperial officer wears the same headgear in gray and the Republic captain (p.9) wears it in blue.

The Naboo security officer's torso piece is unique to him. It features resilient armor plates and a silver-buckled belt

AT-TE Walker (set 4482)

The AT-TE Walker comes with an army of four Phase I clone trooper minifigures, but it can carry up to seven. A gunner operates the swiveling cannon and a driver pilots the vehicle from inside a central cabin.

The Phase I clone trooper is part of a vast army that has been cloned from a single individual. Sealed in a heavy-duty shell of white armor, this minifigure is the first of its kind. During the Clone Wars, clone trooper armor is revised so it is lighter, stronger, and more adaptable.

Blast from the past

The Phase I clone trooper's blaster is a LEGO loudhailer with a translucent blue round plate attached. LEGO *Star Wars* minifigures carried this blaster until bespoke LEGO *Star Wars* blasters were released in 2007.

Only Phase I clone troopers in Episode II sets wear these LEGO helmets

Stripes denote the clone trooper's rank

Blank Head

Phase I clone troopers do not have identities—they have faceless black heads under their LEGO helmets.

DC-15 blaster

Utility belt carries clone trooper survival gear

Clone Trooper
GENETICALLY MODIFIED SOLDIER

DATA FILE

SET: 4482 AT-TE Walker
YEAR: 2003
PIECES: 4
EQUIPMENT: Blaster
VARIANTS: 1

Captain Rex is a clone captain who serves under General Anakin Skywalker in the Battle for Geonosis (set 7869). He is featured in two LEGO sets, also appearing in 2008's AT-TE Walker (set 7675). He is not a typical clone underneath his helmet, as he has a unique LEGO head piece. Rex is heavily armored and carries two blasters making him particularly bold in battle.

Rangefinder assists navigation

Unique clone
Although he is a clone, Rex has his own unique head piece. His face has a 5 o'clock shadow pattern printed on it.

As well as this helmet with blue battle honors, Rex also has a clone trooper visor

Dark bluish-gray pauldron armor to protect the clone trooper's shoulders during intense combat

Rangefinder
Captain Rex's minifigure is almost exactly the same in the two sets he comes in. The only difference is that he wears a dark bluish-gray rangefinder on his helmet in the 2011 set Battle for Geonosis (set 7869).

Bluish-gray blaster pistols

Captain Rex
CLONE TROOPER CAPTAIN

Rex wears an anti-blast kama around his waist that protects most of his legs from close-range blasts

DATA FILE
SET: 7869 Battle for Geonosis
YEAR: 2011
PIECES: 7
EQUIPMENT: Two blaster pistols, pauldron, kama
VARIANTS: 1

Separatist Shuttle (set 8036)

Onaconda Farr is exclusive to this LEGO set. He greets a Separatist shuttle that has landed on Rodia. Nute Gunray, two battle droids, and a pilot battle droid are on board.

They want Onaconda to pledge his support to the Separatists and betray Padmé.

Onaconda Farr is a Senator from the planet Rodia. He is loyal to the Republic and a dear and trusted friend of Senator Padmé Amidala. His minifigure has green Rodian skin, unique blue face markings, and is dressed in his official senatorial robes. Onaconda appears in just one Clone Wars set, where he must choose whether to oppose the Separatists or betray an old friend.

Sensory organs give Rodians exceptional powers of hearing and smell

Rodians have large, glassy eyes that sometimes sparkle

Rodians

Onaconda's head-mold was created initially for bounty hunter Greedo's 2003 minifigure. The same mold was used again for the slave W. Wald in 2011. All three Rodian head pieces have different colors and printing.

Onaconda's unique torso is printed with his senatorial outfit

Onaconda is the only minifigure in LEGO *Star Wars* to have dark purple arm pieces

DATA FILE

SET: 8036 Separatist Shuttle
YEAR: 2009
PIECES: 3
EQUIPMENT: None
VARIANTS: 1

Onaconda's sand-green senatorial pants are made from expensive fabric available only on Rodia

Onaconda Farr
RODIAN SENATOR

Commander Wolffe is the tough leader of the elite Wolfpack clone trooper squad. His minifigure wears a helmet and armor printed with unique Wolfpack insignia and rank markings. Wolffe also has a unique face under his helmet, which sets him apart from the other clones in the LEGO *Star Wars* galaxy.

Clone Commander Wolffe
LEADER OF THE PACK

Rangefinder is connected to a display screen in Wolffe's visor

DATA FILE
SET: 7964 Republic Frigate
YEAR: 2011
PIECES: 6
EQUIPMENT: Twin blaster pistols
VARIANTS: 1

Red and yellow markings designate Wolffe as the unit commander

Stylized wolf design shows squad affiliation

Wolfpack armor is the same as regular clone trooper armor, but with sand-blue markings and sleeves

Battle-scarred
Commander Wolffe has a face with unique scar and stubble printing. He lost his eye in a duel with Asajj Ventress (p160).

DC-17 hand blaster

Kama protects lower body from flying shrapnel

Wolffe's armor
Commander Wolffe's clone armor torso is identical to his squad member, the Wolfpack clone trooper.

Wolffe's legs are sand-blue with white markings painted on top

Ahsoka's Starfighter and Vulture Droid (set 7751)

R7-A7 proves his worth in the one LEGO set he appears in. The plucky droid helps Ahsoka fight off a buzz droid that has latched onto her Delta-7 starfighter.

R7-A7 is a brave astromech droid who helps navigate and repair Ahsoka Tano's starfighter. His minifigure has a dark red body unit and a white head, with lime green and silver access panels. The helpful droid only appears in one LEGO set. R7-A7's brightly colored printing matches Ahsoka's red and green starship, which has a droid socket for him to plug into.

DATA FILE

SET: 7751 Ahsoka's Starfighter and Vulture Droid

YEAR: 2009

PIECES: 4

EQUIPMENT: None

VARIANTS: 1

Head piece is the same mold as other LEGO astromech droids, but the coloring is unique to R7-A7

Logic function display indicates what R7-A7 is thinking

Dark red pins
R7-A7 should be proud of his bright, unique coloring. He is the only astromech droid to have LEGO Technic leg pieces in dark red. In fact, these dark red pin pieces are not found in any other LEGO sets.

R7-A7 has many of the same functions as R2-D2, but he is not quite as intelligent

Astromech droids have two fixed legs and a third retractable leg that is stored inside the unit

Acoustic signaler allows R7-A7 to communicate

Recharge power coupling can be attached to the power source on Ahsoka's starship

R7-A7

AHSOKA'S ASTROMECH

Commander Fox makes only one appearance in the LEGO *Star Wars* galaxy in Separatist Spider Droid (set 7681) in 2008. He is well armed and armored for this battle against the huge, spindly Separatist spider droid. His minifigure has a unique red-patterned torso and helmet.

Rangefinder feeds into a computer screen in Fox's visor

Separatist Spider Droid (set 7681)

The spider droid looks intimidating, but with such long legs, it isn't always stable, so Fox has a chance of winning this mighty battle.

Distinctive helmet with dark red markings instantly identifies Fox

Commander Fox
CLONE TROOPER COMMANDER

Blaster pistol

The red ranking stripes and decoration on Fox's unique torso and helmet represent his deployment on Coruscant

Extra protection

Commander Fox also comes with full shoulder protective armor. His torso has detailed printing on the back.

Dark bluish-gray anti-blast kama leg armor

DATA FILE

SET: 7681 Separatist Spider Droid
PIECES: 7
EQUIPMENT: Two blaster pistols, pauldron, kama
VARIANTS: 1

Geonosian Starfighter (set 7959)

Commander Cody fights alongside Ki-Adi-Mundi in this 2011 LEGO set. They face a Geonosian starfighter, flown by a Geonosian pilot, which is fitted with a rotating cannon and opening cockpit.

Clone Commander Cody leads a battalion of clone troopers and reports to Jedi General Obi-Wan Kenobi. His minifigure wears clone trooper armor that has been modified to reflect Cody's unit and his rank as commander. He has appeared in two LEGO sets since 2008, in which he fights bravely during the Clone Wars.

Visor shield only worn by LEGO *Star Wars* clone commanders

DATA FILE

SET: 7959 Geonosian Starfighter
YEAR: 2011
PIECES: 7
EQUIPMENT: Twin blaster pistols, visor shield, pauldron, kama
VARIANTS: 1

Armor additions

Cody's minifigure comes with a gray pauldron that fits round his neck and a kama leg armor that clips under his torso. These extra pieces of armor designate Cody's rank as commander.

Unique helmet with orange commander markings

Orange markings denote Cody's affiliation with the 212th Attack Battalion

Cody wears the same basic armor as his fellow clone troopers, but his torso has orange arms and extra orange markings

Cody has been trained as an ARC trooper, so he is familiar with a variety of weapons

Commander Cody
OBI-WAN'S CLONE COMMANDER

21

The clone pilot is trained to fly the super-fast Republic and Jedi starships. His minifigure's uniform includes a blue jumpsuit, an armored torso with specialist equipment, and a high-tech helmet with communications system. There are three variants of the clone pilot, each with a different helmet and head piece.

Helmet is marked with red and yellow Republic symbols

STAR VARIANT

Face revealed
The clone pilot of the 2010 ARC-170 Starfighter (set 8088) wears his plain helmet over a flesh-colored face printed with orange visor and chin strap.

Faceless
This original variant flies starships in two sets from 2005–2006. His white, fin-topped helmet covers a plain black head piece, and his torso features blue tubes.

Helmet contains an air filtration system

Torso and legs are the same as Captain Jag's minifigure, but Jag wears a different pilot helmet

DATA FILE
SET: 8096 Emperor Palpatine's Shuttle
YEAR: 2010
PIECES: 4
EQUIPMENT: None
VARIANTS: 3

White airtight flight gloves

Life-support pack integrated into clone pilot uniform—in case of emergency

Clone Pilot
FEARLESS FLIER

Masked pilot
Beneath his helmet, the clone pilot's face is covered by a flight mask. It is printed with breathing holes and a visor.

Contingency plan
The clone pilot needs to be prepared for anything! The back of his torso is printed with a parachute.

STAR VARIANT

Close clone
This clone trooper variant appears in two 2005–2007 LEGO sets. He has no dotted mouth grille pattern on his helmet, and a slightly less detailed torso piece than his 2010 counterpart.

This clone trooper minifigure is wearing advanced Phase II armor. The Phase I design (p.15) has been improved because of feedback received during the Clone Wars, and the minifigure's helmet and torso design now have a different look. This minifigure appears in three Episode III sets.

Phase II clone troopers have blank black heads that can be seen through the open T-visor of their helmets

DATA FILE
SET: 8091 Republic Swamp Speeder
YEAR: 2010
PIECES: 4
EQUIPMENT: Blaster, electrobinoculars
VARIANTS: 2

Heat dispersal vents aid breathing

Detailed torso design is new for the 2010 variant and is only seen on this LEGO minifigure

Phase II clone troopers have carried this blaster gun since 2007

Improvements
The Phase II clone trooper minifigure has been issued with a revised version of the Phase I clone trooper's LEGO helmet. It is a different shape as it contains superior communications and breathing apparatus.

Clone Trooper
GENETICALLY MODIFIED SOLDIER

The **Star Corps** trooper is one of the most skilled soldiers in the LEGO *Star Wars* galaxy. As part of the elite 327th Star Corps, his minifigure wears unique armor with yellow markings. He brings his combat expertise to two LEGO sets: Clone Turbo Tank (set 7261) and Clone Troopers Battle Pack (set 7655).

STAR VARIANT

Top trooper

An orange-and-black LEGO pauldron shows that this Star Corps trooper is a squadron leader. This variant appears in Clone Turbo Tank (set 7261).

Star Corps Trooper
ELITE CLONE TROOPER

Back armor
The back of the Star Corps trooper's torso shows his armor plates, power pack, and black body glove.

A yellow stripe extends from the Star Corps trooper's helmet through his chest armor

This torso piece is only seen on the Star Corps trooper. It features yellow markings and a blaster magazine strap over the right shoulder

A black body glove covers the Star Corps trooper's entire body

The Star Corps trooper carries two of these DC-15S blasters in the Clone Turbo Tank (set 7261)

DATA FILE

SET: 7655 Clone Troopers Battle Pack
YEAR: 2007
PIECES: 4
EQUIPMENT: Blaster
VARIANTS: 2

24

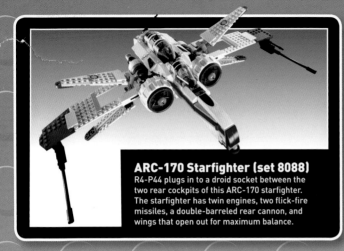

ARC-170 Starfighter (set 8088)
R4-P44 plugs in to a droid socket between the two rear cockpits of this ARC-170 starfighter. The starfighter has twin engines, two flick-fire missiles, a double-barreled rear cannon, and wings that open out for maximum balance.

Green astromech droid
R4-P44 helps with the navigation and repairs on Kit Fisto's ARC-170 Starfighter (set 8088). His minifigure uses the same four LEGO pieces as the other astromech droids in the LEGO *Star Wars* galaxy, but with unique coloring and printed detail. R4-P44 appears in just one LEGO set, where he plays a small but vital part in the Clone Wars.

DATA FILE
SET: 8088 ARC-170 Starfighter
YEAR: 2010
PIECES: 4
EQUIPMENT: None
VARIANTS: 1

Only one other LEGO astromech droid has a blue status display, R2-Q2

Computer interface arm is behind this panel

Panel opens up to reveal the compartment containing R4-P44's manipulator arms

Astromech legs have built-in rocket thrusters

R4-P44
RELIABLE ASTROMECH

The Kashyyyk trooper or "Swamp Trooper" is well-equipped for operations on jungle worlds. He wears custom-made camouflage armor and carries essentials for survival in harsh environments. The minifigure has been called up for action in only one LEGO *Star Wars* set to date.

Kashyyyk Trooper
CAMOUFLAGED CLONE TROOPER

Clone Turbo Tank (set 7261)

The Kashyyyk Trooper flanks the Clone Turbo Tank on his turbine-engine BARC speeder. The speeder has controls for the minifigure to pilot the vehicle with and two blasters on either side of the seat.

Wide visor provides greater visibility in jungle worlds

Scout trooper

The Kashyyyk trooper is part of a scouting unit based in the jungle world of Kashyyyk, so his LEGO helmet is of the same design as the scout trooper minifigure. The scout trooper wears the helmet in white.

This minifigure has a unique torso piece. He wears camouflage armor to blend in with forest and swamp surroundings

Extra utility pockets for jungle survival equipment

Unique printed legs feature ammo pouches

DATA FILE

SET: 7261 Clone Turbo Tank
YEAR: 2005/6
PIECES: 4
EQUIPMENT: Blaster
VARIANTS: 1

Wookiee Attack (set 7258)
Two Wookiee warriors are needed to operate this ornithopter; one pilot and one gunner. A classic example of Wookiee technology, the ornithopter flies into action against an invading dwarf spider droid and amphibious tank during the Battle of Kashyyyk in this set.

You don't want to anger a Wookiee! Although often peaceful and placid, these creatures can become ferocious when attacked. This proud Wookiee warrior minifigure springs to the defense of his homeworld when the Separatists invade Kashyyyk in two 2005 LEGO sets.

Gold-decorated helmet molded as part of head

This minifigure could be based on Tarfful as he also wears a crossed bandolier

DATA FILE
SET: 7260 Wookiee Catamaran
YEAR: 2005
PIECES: 3
EQUIPMENT: Spear
VARIANTS: 1

The Wookiee warrior minifigure comes with this LEGO spear in the Wookiee Catamaran (set 7260)

Emblem indicates clan identity of warrior

Round the back
The reverse side of the warrior's torso repeats the silver and gold bandolier molding, but it is cut short by the back of the helmet.

Wookiee Warrior
DEFENDER OF KASHYYYK

These clone trooper minifigures are highly trained combat specialists. They are the elite forces that carry out vital and dangerous missions for the Grand Army of the Republic, and are seen in only a select few LEGO sets. Each clone trooper specialist wears Phase II LEGO armor with distinguishing colors or equipment.

Clone Troopers
CLONE SPECIALISTS

Shock troopers wear red-emblazoned armor to distinguish them as the elite force on Coruscant

Short blaster gun. Shock troopers also carry blaster rifles for long-range targets

DATA FILE
NAME: Shock trooper
SPECIALTY: Elite Coruscant guard
SET: 7671 AT-AP Walker
YEAR: 2008
PIECES: 4
EQUIPMENT: Blaster, blaster rifle
VARIANTS: 2

The original variant of this minifigure has black hips. It appears in the Clone Troopers Battle Pack (set 7655)

Phase II clone trooper helmet with dark-red markings

Blaster is a LEGO loudhailer with a translucent light-blue round plate

Recon trooper emblem identifies unit

DATA FILE
NAME: Recon trooper
SPECIALTY: Reconnaissance missions
SET: 7250 Clone Scout Walker
YEAR: 2005
PIECES: 4
EQUIPMENT: Blaster
VARIANTS: 1

Audio pick-up for specialist communications

Green markings distinguish this minifigure as part of the 42nd Siege Battalion

Black body glove under white armor

DATA FILE

NAME: Siege Battalion trooper
SPECIALTY: Besieging enemy strongholds
SET: 7260 Wookiee Catamaran
YEAR: 2005
PIECES: 4
EQUIPMENT: Blaster
VARIANTS: 1

Jetpack warhead missiles

Dark visor
Like ordinary clone troopers (p.23), each of these specialized clone troopers has a plain black head, which can be seen through the open visor of his helmet so that the visor appears black.

The aerial trooper is the only minifigure to utilize this black flag LEGO piece

DATA FILE

NAME: Aerial trooper
SPECIALTY: Airborne assaults
SET: 7261 Clone Turbo Tank
YEAR: 2005/6
PIECES: 16
EQUIPMENT: Jetpack, sniper rifle
VARIANTS: 1

Super-size sniper rifle

DK | Penguin Random House

Editors Hannah Dolan, Shari Last,
Victoria Taylor, and Matt Jones
Designers Anne Sharples and Jon Hall
Senior Producer Lloyd Robertson
Senior DTP Designer David McDonald
Managing Editor Simon Hugo
Design Manager Guy Harvey
Creative Manager Sarah Harland
Art Director Lisa Lanzarini
Publisher Julie Ferris
Publishing Director Simon Beecroft

Additional minifigures photographed by Huw Millington,
Ace Kim, Jeremy Beckett, and Tony Wood

First published in the United States in 2015
by DK Publishing
345 Hudson Street, New York, New York 10014

Contains material previously published in
LEGO® Star Wars® Character Encyclopedia (2011)

004-284485-Feb/15

Page design copyright ©2015 Dorling Kindersley Limited
A Penguin Random House Company

A catalog record for this book is available from
the Library of Congress.

ISBN: 978-5-0010-1297-9

Color reproduction by Media Development Printing Ltd, UK
Printed and bound in China

Dorling Kindersley would like to thank:
Jonathan W. Rinzler, Troy Alders, Rayne Roberts, Pablo
Hidalgo, and Leland Chee at Lucasfilm; Stephanie
Lawrence, Randi Sørensen, Lisbeth Langjkær, Jens
Kronvold Frederiksen, Chris Bonven Johansen, and John
McCormack at the LEGO Group; LEGO Star Wars
collectors Ace Kim and Huw Millington; Emma Grange,
Lisa Stock, Sarah Harland, Ellie Hallsworth, and Nicola
Brown for editorial support; and Owen Bennett for
design support on the cover.

www.dk.com
www.LEGO.com
www.starwars.com

A WORLD OF IDEAS:
SEE ALL THERE IS TO KNOW